Impact The World

SUCCESS
TIPS FOR
SPEAKERS

**50 Tips
To Jump-Start Your Speaking Career**

D1519270

CHERYL WOOD

ISBN #: 978-1-5323-6364-1

ENGAGING. ENERGETIC. THOUGHT-PROVOKING.

THE IDEAL
PROFESSIONAL SPEAKER
FOR YOUR NEXT EVENT!

Any organization, association, or group that is seeking a fresh, new perspective on topics related to personal and professional development, accompanied by an infectious energy that will motivate your group to become peak performers who refuse to play small, needs to hire Cheryl for a keynote and/or workshop training!

**TO <u>BOOK</u> CHERYL TO SPEAK OR
TO <u>HIRE</u> CHERYL FOR SPEAKER TRAINING, CONTACT:**

(301) 395-7589
Assistant@Cherylwoodempowers.com
www.CherylWoodEmpowers.com

This book is dedicated to individuals globally who are bold enough to share their unique voice, perspective, message, and story with the world to create positive impact!

CONTENTS

Introduction
Speaker Tip #1: Be Ready
Speaker Tip #2: Know Your Message
Speaker Tip #3: Know Your Audience
Speaker Tip #4: Know Your Fee
Speaker Tip #5: Open With A Bang
Speaker Tip #6: Shift Your Energy
Speaker Tip #7: Meet The Expectation
Speaker Tip #8: Distinguish Your Work
Speaker Tip #9: Stop Being "FREE"
Speaker Tip #10: Share Compelling Stories
Speaker Tip #11: Develop Confidence
Speaker Tip #12: Eliminate Filler Words
Speaker Tip #13: Be Conversational
Speaker Tip #14: Do Not Overwhelm
Speaker Tip #15: Use Eye Contact
Speaker Tip #16: Deliver Real Value
Speaker Tip #17: Incorporate Pauses
Speaker Tip #18: Be Well Organized
Speaker Tip #19: Close With Fireworks
Speaker Tip #20: Demonstrate The 3-C's
Speaker Tip #21: Do Your Research
Speaker Tip #22: Be Intentional
Speaker Tip #23: Use Powerpoint To Enhance
Speaker Tip #24: Put It In Writing
Speaker Tip #25: Speak To Many
Speaker Tip #26: Go Global
Speaker Tip #27: Don't Wait, CREATE
Speaker Tip #28: Share Your Signature Story
Speaker Tip #29: Demonstrate Integrity
Speaker Tip #30: Be An Original

Speaker Tip #31: Be Versatile
Speaker Tip #32: Arrive Early
Speaker Tip #33: Don't "Wing It"
Speaker Tip #34: Pace Yourself
Speaker Tip #35: Abandon the Podium
Speaker Tip #36: Do Not Assume
Speaker Tip #37: Know The Numbers
Speaker Tip #38: Keep In Touch
Speaker Tip #39: Record Attendee Testimonials
Speaker Tip #40: Customize and Personalize It
Speaker Tip #41: Create Products
Speaker Tip #42: Be Relatable
Speaker Tip #43: Grow Your Visibility
Speaker Tip #44: Diversify Your Revenue
Speaker Tip #45: Be Passionate
Speaker Tip #46: Keep Learning
Speaker Tip #47: Create Relevant Titles
Speaker Tip #48: Believe In Your Value
Speaker Tip #49: Follow The Formula
Speaker Tip #50: Think Abundantly
Congratulations
Next Steps

INTRODUCTION

As I humbly reflect on the growth I've experienced in my career as a professional speaker, it never ceases to amaze me what you can accomplish when you set your mind to something, develop insurmountable belief in your ability to accomplish it, and consistently execute the work to make it a reality.

I vividly remember the start of my speaking career and my very first speaking engagement on September 18, 2010 at Morgan State University (MSU) in Baltimore, Maryland. On that day, I was extended the opportunity to speak at MSU's Annual W.O.M.E.N. Conference to teach other moms how to start their own businesses. I will never forget how nervous I was. And even though it was an unpaid speaking engagement, I still felt completely unqualified to be the person at the front of the room who was viewed as the expert. I initially thought to myself, "I don't have enough experience to be a speaker. Nobody knows who I am. Nobody will ever value my advice. I'm just an inexperienced wanna-be. There are so many other speakers who are better than me." I had totally disqualified myself before I ever took the stage! Boy oh Boy did I have a lot to learn. And over the course of time, one of the biggest lessons I learned was this: "even when

you don't feel *qualified*, it doesn't mean you haven't been *called*."
Ultimately, I discovered that I was *called* to speak, that it was the thing I was BORN TO DO. Speaking was my unique gift that would allow me to leave my unique fingerprint on the world, and it was the one career I had embarked upon throughout the course of my adult life that finally brought me an insurmountable sense of purpose, joy, and internal fulfillment.

So, let me ask you: Do you have a similar passion for speaking? Is there a message embedded inside of you that you feel deeply compelled to share with others? Do you become energized whenever you think about sharing your message because you know it gives others hope and inspires them to play bigger in life? Is there a topic you have extensive experience and knowledge in that you want to use to educate others so they can live more productively? Have you been holding yourself back from sharing your message because you feel unqualified? Do you feel stuck because you're unsure of the steps you need to take to jump-start your speaking career? Do you believe there are already too many people speaking on the topic you want to speak on? Have you convinced yourself that there are not enough speaking opportunities for you to get a piece of the pie?

Well, allow me to interrupt any and all negative self-talk that you might currently be engaged in about your ability, or the available opportunities, to become an impactful, highly sought-after, highly paid speaker who transforms lives. Hear me loud and clear: There are over 7.6 Billion people on the planet and somebody needs to know what you know right now! You have everything it takes to impact their lives with your message!

One word of caution, whatever your reason for pursing speaking, I beckon you to be the best that you can be at it. Whether you feel that it is a "gift" or it is simply a skill set that you want to develop, give yourself permission to deliver the best performance possible on every platform, for every engagement by investing the time and energy to **master** the craft. Make a commitment to take the craft seriously and acknowledge the great responsibility that comes with speaking into people's lives. After all, every audience that you have the privilege of speaking to deserves your very best!

Even though I consider speaking to be my "gift", I still acknowledge the importance of **mastering** the craft so that I'm able to make the greatest impact possible. And since 2010, mastering the craft of speaking has paid off in a big way. Not only have I been blessed to positively impact thousands of lives globally – in over 30 states in the United States and as far away as India, United Kingdom, and Bahamas, speaking at organizations including The United Nations, Federal Bureau of Investigations (FBI), United States Department of Defense, United States Department of Agriculture, Verizon, National Association of Legal Professionals, International Association of Administrative Professionals, Federally Employed Women, and Blacks In Government – but I was also able to walk away from my full-time job as a legal secretary of 15 years to become a highly sought-after, highly paid international motivational speaker. I'm not any different than you. Whatever your big speaking goal is, you are enough to make it manifest!!

Another big lesson I learned in my journey as a speaker is to "say yes more than you say no." You open yourself up to greater opportunities and to exponential growth. By saying "yes" to that first speaking opportunity at MSU in 2010 – and many opportunities afterwards that I still didn't feel qualified for at that time – I shifted the trajectory of my life and learned what I was truly capable of. Think about it, there is no way you can learn what you're capable of when you constantly run in the opposite direction of opportunities simply because they scare you. I've discovered that the best way to grow, develop your skills, and build greater confidence as a speaker is to accept as many opportunities to challenge yourself as possible.

After you say "yes", then you have to become intentional. Following my first speaking engagement in 2010, I became intentional about actively seeking the speaking opportunities I desired from that point forward. I always allowed the words, *"You never get what you deserve, you get what you demand"* to ring in my ears to remind me that I had to keep showing up and working for what I wanted. No one was going to hand it to me. I had to learn that you must "plant so many seeds that you lose count." And, it will pay off.

So, stop and ask yourself now, "how bad do I really want to share my voice as a speaker?" If it's truly worth having, surely it's worth working for. Begin implementing the following **50 Success Tips for Speakers** and continue to fuel your possibilities on a daily basis. Commit to the full journey and do not abandon ship even in the face of challenges, setbacks, and obstacles. The journey won't be perfect but it will be worth it. Keep expressing belief in your unique voice and allow this book to serve as a valuable resource to support you along the journey.

SPEAKER TIP #1:

BE READY

SPEAKER TIP #1:

The best thing you can do to succeed as a speaker is to **Be Ready** to present yourself to the world instead of having to **Get Ready**! Start by laying a solid speaker foundation so you never have to turn down an opportunity because you're not ready. Put the fundamentals below in place immediately:

- Professional Headshots (2-3 poses)
- Professional Website
- Speaker One Sheet or Media Kit
- Social Media Sites (try to set-up your sites with the same handle and be actively engaged)
- Customer Relationship Management (CRM) Tool (this is your database to store contact information of those who OPT-IN to stay connected to you)
- Speaker Bio (have a brief bio of 100-150 words and a full bio)Å
- Speaker Introduction (75-word introduction of how you want to be introduce to the stage)
- Speaker Reel
- YouTube Channel

SPEAKER TIP #2:

KNOW YOUR MESSAGE

SPEAKER TIP #2:

Take the time to get crystal clear about what your core message is as a professional speaker and determine how your message will impact the audiences who hear you speak. One of your biggest assets as a speaker is being able to clearly articulate your message, your solutions, and your value. Reflect on the top 5 questions to unveil your core message:

1. Who am I and what have I been through in my life that will be relatable to a specific audience? Who is that audience I most want to impact?

2. What did I overcome and how (specific steps)?

3. What did I learn along the way (strategies/tips/tools)?

4. What did I succeed at and what results did I achieve?

5. What am I going to teach my audience that they can implement NOW to make their lives better?

SPEAKER TIP #3:

KNOW YOUR AUDIENCE

SPEAKER TIP #3:

Avoid one of the biggest mistakes made by speakers entering the speaking industry: **trying to appeal to EVERYONE**. Instead, clarify exactly who you want to serve, what their problem is, and what your solution is. Narrowing down a niche does not mean you cannot service individuals outside of that niche, it simply means you have a clearly identified message and solution for a specific audience that you intend to target in your marketing efforts. Consider the following:

- The audience I can add the MOST value to consistently is...
- The topic(s) I have the MOST knowledge and experience in to best serve this audience is...
- The information MOST frequently requested by this audience is...
- The topic that brings me the MOST joy in presenting is...

SPEAKER TIP #4:

KNOW YOUR FEE

SPEAKER TIP #4:

Familiarize yourself with the various speaker platforms and KNOW YOUR SPEAKERS FEE for each. It is important that you have a set fee schedule and that you are ready to confidently state your fee when asked. Do not fumble and try to make up a fee on the spot. Practice stating your fee, but also be willing and ready to negotiate.

KEYNOTE: The main speech at a conference, convention, or event. Keynote speakers generally command higher fees and typically speak for 30-60 minutes.

BREAKOUT: A session that is part of a track that other speakers are booked on. Most sessions are 45-90 minutes and multiple breakout sessions are held simultaneously. Attendance is less than at keynotes.

PANEL: A group of experts who gather simultaneously to discuss a topic. Experts may have differing viewpoints and wide perspectives. Speakers have less time to speak, so keep your responses clear and concise.

WORKSHOP: A presentation on a specific subject matter that offers a greater degree of attendee participation, interaction, and hands-on exercises. A workshop can span from 45-minutes to a half or full day.

SPEAKER TIP #5:

OPEN WITH A BANG

SPEAKER TIP #5:

Open every presentation with a BANG! A BANG denotes an opening that sparks intrigue and interest in what you are about to say. For every audience and every platform, take the time to develop a powerful "**SEYD Opening**" **(Stop Everything You're Doing Opening)**. Your opening should move your audience to drop everything they're doing and abandon everything else they're thinking about to fully tune into your message. This is critical because your opening will capture the attention of your audience or create disinterest. The success of your **SEYD Opening** is dependent upon *what* you say and *how* you say it. Decide on your **SEYD Opening** and OWN IT! Ask yourself:

- Will I share a short story?
- Will I tell a joke?
- Will I reveal a jaw-dropping statistic?
- Will I have the audience repeat a mantra?
- Will I get the audience out of their seats dancing?

SPEAKER TIP #6:

SHIFT YOUR ENERGY

SPEAKER TIP #6:

Nervousness has the ability to prevent you from delivering your best presentation and from enjoying the message you are delivering. You owe it to yourself and your audience to shift your nervousness into positive energy. If you feel nervous before going onto stage, be intentional about redirecting the nervous energy through your body as positive energy – move around and jab your arms like a boxer; take long, slow, deep meditation-type breaths; dance to your favorite song; sing out loud; laugh heartily; or execute any movement that makes you feel more relaxed, more courageous, and ready to show up powerfully and confidently when you step onto the stage. Remember, the audience is rooting for your success… you just have to relax and deliver!

SPEAKER TIP #7:

MEET THE EXPECTATION

SPEAKER TIP #7:

Your biggest area of focus as a speaker is never whether or not you receive the loudest applause or a standing ovation... it is whether or not you **fully meet the expectation of the planner/organizer who hired you**. The planner/organizer can likely rehire you for future opportunities and can also connect you to other decision makers who can hire you. Be intentional about assessing their expectation before the event, ask for their feedback onsite after you speak, and always schedule a post-event call to request their feedback about your performance.

Steps for the post-event call with the planner/organizer:
- Recap the expectation that was discussed on the PRE-event call and share what you most enjoyed about the opportunity.
- Ask: What did you value most about the presentation?
- Ask: What, if anything, could have added greater value?
- Ask: Are you willing to refer me to three other organizations who would equally benefit from this presentation?

NOTE: Consider handing out brief evaluations to attendees, collecting them, and sending the feedback from the evaluations to the organizer before your post-event call.

SPEAKER TIP #8:

DISTINGUISH
YOUR WORK

SPEAKER TIP #8:

As a professional speaker, it is important that you distinguish the difference between your "*Heart Work*" and your "*Wealth Work*". Your *Heart Work* allows you to serve those you deeply care about but who may not be in a position to pay for your services. *Heart Work* is done on your own terms with the understanding that you are serving without expectation. On the other hand, your *Wealth Work* is specifically about revenue generation and profit margins. Your *Wealth Work* should always position you to magnetize individuals who want the solutions you offer and who have the disposable income to invest in it now. Take the time to distinguish and separate the two so you don't remain a 'starving speaker' who loves what you do but stays broke doing it. Reflect on the following:

- Who is my *Heart Work* audience?
- Who is my *Wealth Work* audience?

SPEAKER TIP #9:

STOP BEING "FREE"

SPEAKER TIP #9:

You are never "FREE" as a professional speaker. When you get booked to speak, you should expect to *deliver* value and you should expect to *gain* value. If the organization that books you does not have a budget, you can opt to "waive your fee" but still position yourself for a monetary win. The secret: Be sure to ask the planner or organizer specific questions about the audience you will be serving and determine whether or not they **want** the solutions you provide. If they **want** your solutions, you can still generate your full speakers fee from a sales offer. Request that the organization offer you the opportunity to sell your offerings from the stage. This will position you to generate your full speakers fee or more.

EXAMPLE:
Your Speakers Fee: $5,000 (waived your fee) = $0.00
Your Virtual Program Sold From Stage: $597 x 10 Sales = $5,970
Your Books Sold At Event: $20 x 50 Books = $1,000
TOTAL GENERATED: $6,970 (MORE than your speakers fee)

SPEAKER TIP #10:

SHARE COMPELLING STORIES

SPEAKER TIP #10:

The best speakers are those who share compelling stories that support their talking points. To uniquely brand yourself in the speaker marketplace, take the time to identify your *signature story* and your *supporting* stories. What's the difference? Your *signature story* is your life story that identifies the struggles, choices, challenges, triumphs, process, results, and outcome that is most closely related to the subject matter and solutions you speak about. Your *signature story* does not change – it is the story that ultimately brands who you are as a speaker! On the other hand, *supporting stories* are stories that add breath and life to your speech but will oftentimes change based on your talking points for an event or the audience you are serving at an event.

SPEAKER TIP #11:

DEVELOP CONFIDENCE

SPEAKER TIP #11:

Confidence is an integral part of success in the speaking industry – confidence in yourself, confidence in your message, confidence in your solutions, and confidence that you are qualified to be the expert standing at the front of the room delivering the message. Confidence is demonstrated in everything from your words, tone, volume, pace, posture, gestures, and facial expressions. Your confidence is greatly connected to your belief, so if your confidence as a speaker is wavering reflect on the following questions:

- Do I believe in the message I am delivering?
- Do I believe my message will impact & transform lives?
- Do I believe the solutions I am sharing are viable?
- Have I achieved results from the solutions I am sharing?
- Have I practiced and prepared for this opportunity?

If you can answer **YES** to all of these questions, rest assured that **YOU ARE READY FOR THE PLATFORM!**

SPEAKER TIP #12:

ELIMINATE FILLER WORDS

SPEAKER TIP #12:

Eliminate filler words such as "um" "ah" "er" "like" and "right" from your speeches. These words become a major distraction to your message and typically cause the audience to focus more on *how* you are articulating the message instead of the overall benefit of the message. Most times, filler words are the result of a speaker succumbing to the temptation to fill the silence in-between ideas. Instead of blurting out filler words to fill silence or a loss of your thoughts, slow down, take a moment to organize your thoughts, get comfortable with a brief pause, then continue. Remember, you are only as good as your last performance, so take every speaking opportunity seriously as though it was your last opportunity to make a great impression and lasting impact!

SPEAKER TIP #13:

BE CONVERSATIONAL

SPEAKER TIP #13:

To become an impactful speaker, deliver your content in a conversational tone instead of making the audience feel like you're lecturing or scolding them with a long list of Do's and Dont's. Audiences tend to let their guard down and engage more when they feel that you are speaking **WITH** them instead of **AT** them. A few ways to demonstrate that you are speaking **WITH** an audience is to incorporate the following:

- Incorporate less "I" statements and more "We" and "Us" statements throughout your presentation.

- Use shorter sentences as you would naturally use when talking in a one-on-one conversation with an individual.

- Use rhetorical questions to enhance the sense of conversation.

SPEAKER TIP #14:

DO NOT OVERWHELM

SPEAKER TIP #14:

Do not overwhelm your audience with too much content! Instead, share bite-sized, digestible chunks of information so your audience can retain the "meat" of your presentation. Get into the practice of sharing a few main talking points and apply the **"3E Rule"** to each: Explore, Explain, Elaborate.

- **EXPLORE** a new idea or thought you want them to consider.
- **EXPLAIN** why implementing the idea or thought is important.
- **ELABORATE** on how they can incorporate the idea to make their own lives better.

In the speaking industry, **less is more** – the less you overwhelm the audience with too many ideas, the more your content will stick with them and remain at the forefront of their minds long after you have left the stage.

SPEAKER TIP #15:

USE EYE CONTACT

SPEAKER TIP #15:

Eye contact is a powerful tool that can be used to make a deeper connection with your audience and enhance your impact. Eye contact can persuade your audience to see things as you see them and to make a decision to try the method, idea, or solutions you have presented. Effective eye contact will build rapport with the audience and make individuals feel like you are speaking "directly to them" versus speaking broadly to the entire group. Eye contact makes your speech feel more like a conversation and causes the audience to feel a greater sense of engagement. Whereas, a lack of eye contact can signify lack of confidence, lack of belief, and lack of authority. The rule of thumb for eye contact is: **3-5 seconds before it becomes a stare**.

SPEAKER TIP #16:

DELIVER REAL VALUE

SPEAKER TIP #16:

Making great impact as a speaker is not about getting on stage to prove how smart you are or how much you know. Rather, every platform is an opportunity for you to **deliver valuable content that helps your audience to improve some aspect of their lives** (i.e. career, business, health, image, relationships, productivity). For every speaking opportunity be sure to deliver real value by sharing a range of ideas, including: something they don't already know, something that serves as a reminder, something that propels them into deeper thought, and something that inspires them to want to keep growing. Reflect on this:

- A *new idea or viewpoint* I can present on my topic is…
- A *reminder* I can share on my topic is…
- A *thought-provoking question* I can ask about my topic is…
- An *inspiring story or quote* I can share on my topic is…

SPEAKER TIP #17:

INCORPORATE PAUSES

SPEAKER TIP #17:

There is power in a **PAUSE**. Many speakers master the ability to move an audience through high energy, but most do <u>not</u> master the ability to equally move an audience by allowing the room to get completely quiet by means of a pause. To make greater impact as a speaker, find the one or two pivotal moments during your presentation where silence makes a greater, deeper impact than any words you can express. A pause can be used to:

- get the audience's attention
- transition to a new idea
- make a talking point more dramatic
- give the audience time to fully absorb a thought you have expressed

NOTE: Do not underestimate the use of pauses in every presentation... but do not abuse them!

SPEAKER TIP #18:

BE WELL ORGANIZED

SPEAKER TIP #18:

Every speech you prepare must be well organized to make the greatest impact. Take the time to structure your speeches in a cohesive, logical flow that your audience can easily follow. If your speech title promises to identify a specific number of steps, strategies, or takeaways to achieve a certain result, be cognizant of organizing your speech accordingly and, during your speech, express where you are in the chronological order of your delivery as you transition from one step to the next step (for example, state: "Now, we are moving to step #2"). It is critical that your audience is able to keep up with your steps/keys/strategies so they don't miss critical content. At the conclusion of your speech, be sure to go back and repeat each step again.

SPEAKER TIP #19:

CLOSE WITH FIREWORKS

SPEAKER TIP #19:

The way you close your speech is equally as important as the way you open your speech and should be equally as compelling. To **Close With Fireworks** denotes that your closing should reignite the same energy you ignited when you opened your speech. It should remind the audience of why they invested time in listening to your message. You can choose to close with a powerful mantra, a short story, or even a "Call To Question."

EXAMPLE OF CLOSING:

A "Call to Question" is a rhetorical question that leaves the audience thinking about the impact of the ideas discussed on their lives based on what actions they incorporate and leaves them in deeper thought, for example:

"So, what choice will you make when you leave here today? Will you [insert an idea of change], or will you simply return to your normal routine? The choice is yours!"

SPEAKER TIP #20:

DEMONSTRATE THE 3-C'S

SPEAKER TIP #20:

From the moment you step on stage, your verbal and non-verbal communication must demonstrate the **3-C's**: Confidence, Competence, and Credibility.

CONFIDENCE:

I am comfortable being on stage as the identified expert.

COMPETENCE:

I am knowledgeable and experienced in this subject matter.

CREDIBILITY:

I know my message is relevant to this audience and the solutions I will present are viable.

SPEAKER TIP #21:

DO YOUR RESEARCH

SPEAKER TIP #21:

Always research the organization and the audience before every speaking engagement. Prior to the event, ask the planner/organizer critical questions about the demographics of the audience. Inquire about the audience's knowledge level on the subject matter to be discussed and dig deeper to learn more about the organization or group itself. For example, if you are presenting at an industry event, research the event website and familiarize yourself with the mission of the event. If you are presenting to a corporation, learn as much as you can about the corporation's vision by visiting their website, reading press releases, and reviewing their blogs. Then, incorporate brief snippets of these into your speech. Research and Preparation are a must! Consider:

- Is the company currently celebrating a big win or achievement?
- Is the company currently recovering from a challenge or loss?
- What are general challenges currently faced by the industry?
- How does your message align with the company's vision?

SPEAKER TIP #22:

BE INTENTIONAL

SPEAKER TIP #22:

Be intentional about the speaking engagements you accept. Every speaking engagement might not be the "right fit" for you. As much time and effort as it takes to build a solid reputation as a credible speaker, you do not want to ruin that reputation by accepting a speaking engagement that is out of your wheelhouse and results in a flop. Always remember, you are only as good as your last performance. Avoid saying "yes" just because the opportunity is one that you <u>want</u>. Instead, only say "yes" when you are confident that you are the subject matter expert who is qualified for the opportunity and you have the knowledge base to exceed the planner's expectations and deliver an unforgettable presentation.

NOTE: Make it a point to stay connected to other credible speakers and institute a "finders fee" for referring speaking engagements to them that might not be a good fit for you.

SPEAKER TIP #23:

USE POWERPOINT TO ENHANCE

SPEAKER TIP #23:

Avoid relying on a Powerpoint presentation to do the talking for you. An impactful speaker does not **depend** upon Powerpoint slides or technology for their presentation, rather, they use it to **enhance** their presentation. Remember, your audience did not come to sit and watch you read your Powerpoint slides word for word. **Rule of Thumb:** Keep your Powerpoint slides to a minimum, use large fonts, limit the amount of text on each slide, and incorporate the use of images to drive home your talking points. Use your Powerpoint slides as "sign posts" that signal where you are in your presentation.

NOTE: Know your Powerpoint slides like the back of your hand and practice them enough to be able to deliver the presentation with or without them. At some point in your speaking career you will likely find yourself in a situation where an unexpected technology glitch prevents use of your Powerpoint. Be Ready to present anyway!!

SPEAKER TIP #24:

PUT IT IN WRITING

SPEAKER TIP #24:

Treat your speaking career like a business… because it is a business! This includes putting everything in writing. Always use a legally binding Speaker Agreement to confirm your date to speak, speaker's fee, required deposit amount, dates of balances to be paid, and cancellation policy. Do not lock-in a date until you have received a fully executed Speaker Agreement.

Your Speaker Agreement should also include:

- Event theme and title of your presentation
- Expenses, travel, and transportation arrangements
- On-site point of contact and phone number
- Cancellation Penalty Policy
- Special speaker on-site requests
- Amount of time you are requested to speak
- How long you are requested to remain at the event
- Additional activities you are requested to attend

SPEAKER TIP #25:

SPEAK TO MANY

SPEAKER TIP #25:

There are two types of speakers: (i) Speakers who *love* the stage and (ii) speakers who *leverage* the stage. Even if you don't love the stage, it benefits you to accept the responsibility of impacting as many lives as possible with your message through the platform of speaking. The speakers who become the most successful are those who understand and embrace the power of the one-to-many model versus the one-to-one model, and who are willing to face their fears about public speaking. The one-to-many model dictates that you will have the opportunity to touch more lives by getting in front of groups of people simultaneously than you will speaking to individuals one at a time. Speaking using the one-to-many model will drastically increase your impact and your revenue.

SPEAKER TIP #26:

GO GLOBAL

SPEAKER TIP #26:

Your message has the power to transform people's lives, not just locally but GLOBALLY. Do not allow yourself to get stuck only seeking and accepting speaking opportunities in your own zip code. Instead, seek opportunities outside of your zip code. Exercise a willingness to go into spaces that are new, uncomfortable, and unfamiliar in order to expand your reach. (#GetOnAnAirplane)

Create A Plan of Action:

- How many local speaking events will I secure in the next 12 months? (make a list of the events)
- How many events outside of my zip code will I secure in the next 12 months? (make a list of the events)

SPEAKER TIP #27:

DON'T WAIT, CREATE

SPEAKER TIP #27:

Don't wait, CREATE! As a professional speaker with a desire to get your message out to the masses, you do not have the luxury of sitting and waiting for someone else to offer you a platform to speak on. Instead, take the initiative to **create your own platform**. Oftentimes, taking a bet on yourself can yield greater results than waiting on someone else to take a bet on you. Just remember, when creating your own platform, **do not be afraid to start small**. Don't add the unnecessary pressure of trying to create a platform with hundreds of participants before you are first willing to start with a platform of a few (25-50 participants). Give yourself permission to embrace small beginnings and to grow as you develop increased visibility and credibility. Consider:

- If I host my own live event, what audience will I target? What will be the theme? When will I host it? Where will I host it?
- What are the total expenses of hosting the event?
- Can I collaborate with another influencer to host a live event or a virtual event to share my voice as I build my platform?

SPEAKER TIP #28:

SHARE YOUR SIGNATURE STORY

SPEAKER TIP #28:

Facts, figures, and statistics are important in a speech, but your signature story is equally as important. The data you share in your speeches will make a *head-to-head connection* with your audience that will educate and inform them, but your signature story will have a lasting impact that will leave your audience reflecting on your message long after you leave the stage and will move them to take action after the speech. Your signature story will create a *heart-to-heart connection* that is deeper than any facts, figures, or statistics. Make it a rule to never leave a stage without sharing your signature story! Be sure to incorporate it regardless of how much time you have on stage. Remember, your audience can find facts, figures, and statistics online and in books... but they won't find your story there!

REFLECTION: My Signature Story is... [insert the story you will share repeatedly from every stage, even 20 years from now].

SPEAKER TIP #29:

DEMONSTRATE
INTEGRITY

SPEAKER TIP #29:

Integrity is critical for professional speakers. One way to demonstrate integrity is to always give proper credit to the author of a quote or the creator of an idea that you use, reference, or share during your speeches. Do not make the mistake of taking credit for something you did not create, develop, write, or originate. A good reputation is hard to build as a speaker but easy to destroy.

NOTE: Make it a habit to create your own personal quotes that will resonate with other speakers who will ultimately share them in their speeches.

My five personal quotes that I will heavily share over the next 12 months are:

Quote #1: " _____ "

Quote #2: " _____ "

Quote #3: " _____ "

Quote #4: " _____ "

Quote #5: " _____ "

SPEAKER TIP #30:

BE AN ORIGINAL

SPEAKER TIP #30:

Copying another speaker's content and/or style of delivery is <u>not</u> a compliment! YOU ARE AN ORIGINAL, SO BE ORIGINAL! Express yourself in a way that is unique and authentic to you, your knowledge, and your life lessons learned as a speaker. Find your unique voice and style and **OWN IT**!

1. What adjectives best describe my unique speaking style?
2. What makes my delivery different from any other speaker?
3. What <u>type</u> of speaker do I categorize myself as?
   Educational: a content speaker who can talk on specific subjects in a manner that is educational and informative.
   Inspirational: a speaker who has accomplished something against great odds and shares their life story.
   Motivational: a you-can-do-it speaker who gets a group enthused while providing a message that is useful.
   Industry: a speaker with expertise or a reputation in a specific area of value to a specific audience.
   Celebrity: a well-known personality from the world of sports, entertainment, media, or successful business.

SPEAKER TIP #31:

BE VERSATILE

SPEAKER TIP #31:

Every audience that you speak to will include individuals who have a variety of learning styles. It is your responsibility to be versatile and incorporate components that effectively impact all three core learning styles:

Auditory (Hearing)

Lecture/Oral Presentation
Group Discussions
Sounds

Visual (Seeing)

Graphics
Illustrations
Pictures

Kinesthetic (Doing)

Hands-On Activities
Role Playing
Note Taking

SPEAKER TIP #32:

ARRIVE EARLY

SPEAKER TIP #32:

Make it a habit to arrive at your speaking engagements a minimum of 45-minutes to 1-hour prior to your speaking time. Arriving early will position you to:

- Avoid rushing to the stage in a frazzled state in the event you encounter unforeseen occurrences in route to the engagement
- Assess the overall climate of the environment
- Hear one or two speakers before you speak to make sure you are bringing a fresh perspective
- Meet and greet attendees before you take the stage

NOTE: When you meet and connect with attendees prior to your speech, you no longer feel like you are talking to a room full of strangers when you take the stage.

SPEAKER TIP #33:

DON'T "WING IT"

SPEAKER TIP #33:

Every speech you deliver must be treated as a priority!
After every speech you give, do a self-assessment and
ask yourself "did I give the best of myself to this audience
and this opportunity?" Did I prepare and practice well in
advance? Was I clear about the content I wanted to
deliver or did I just "wing it"? Remember, you are in the
"life-changing and life-transformation" business, so no
matter how long you have been a speaker or what level of
success you have achieved as a speaker, you owe it to
your audience to never "skimp" on a speech. Your
audience always deserves your best delivery possible!

SPEAKER TIP #34:

PACE YOURSELF

SPEAKER TIP #34:

Developing the "art of pace" can be one of your greatest assets as a speaker. Pace is the rate at which you express your ideas and communicate with your audience. If your pace is too **fast** for too long, attendees will become disinterested because they won't be able to keep up and will feel that they're missing out on pertinent ideas. If your pace is too **slow** for too long, the speech will become monotone and boring to attendees and they will become distracted by other things. Your goal should be to speak at a conversational pace for the bulk of your speech, and periodically incorporate fast and slow pace periods.

FAST: can indicate passion, excitement, energy, or emotion

SLOW: can indicate importance, seriousness of a talking point, or sadness

SPEAKER TIP #35:

ABANDON THE PODIUM

SPEAKER TIP #35:

Avoid standing behind a podium to deliver your speech (unless the organizer absolutely requires podium use due to the stage set-up or videography requirements). When you stand behind a podium, you create a physical barrier between you and the audience. A podium interferes with the audience's plain sight of view as you deliver your speech – your full expressions, including eye contact and body language – and minimizes your level of engagement. Furthermore, for most speakers, a podium automatically encourages bad posture (leaning or clutching onto the podium), discourages natural hand gestures, makes your speech feel more like a lecture than a conversation, and encourages reading your speech directly from an outline or script. Come from behind the podium and watch how your audience engagement drastically increases!

SPEAKER TIP #36:

DO NOT ASSUME

SPEAKER TIP #36:

To become a successful speaker, do not assume that everyone in your audience is starting from scratch. It is your responsibility to research your audience and ask questions about your audience before you take the stage in order to be fully aware of their knowledge level on the topic you will be presenting. You do not want to insult your audience by presenting novice content and ideas to advanced learners (or vice versa). Make time to speak to the planner/organizer prior to the event to find out if the audience has a beginner, intermediate, or advanced level of knowledge about your topic, then prepare your content accordingly.

SPEAKER TIP #37:

KNOW THE NUMBERS

SPEAKER TIP #37:

For every speaking engagement, inquire about the number of people who will be in attendance at the event and the layout of the room. There are subtle differences you can tweak in your presentation when speaking to an intimate group of 30 versus speaking to a large group of 300. Being aware of the expected number of attendees can be instrumental in determining what visual aids you use, knowing how much space you have to physically engage with the audience, what activities you can or cannot incorporate based on the number of participants, how much you will need to project your voice, and other physical aspects of your presentation. Always know the numbers!

SPEAKER TIP #38:

KEEP IN TOUCH

SPEAKER TIP #38:

Your speech is only <u>one</u> touch point for people to experience you. It is important that you provide alternative ways for attendees in your audience to connect and continue their experience with you beyond your 45-60 minute speech. Consider the following options:

- Create a content-rich handout for attendees to take home and make sure the handout contains your contact and social media information.

- Distribute fun promotional items as takeaways and make sure the items "brand" your company and contain your contact information.

- Create a FREE, JUICY offer as a giveaway through text-message marketing that will automatically connect attendees to your CRM (never add people to your database without their permission, so clearly articulate that those who opt-in will become a part of your database).

SPEAKER TIP #39:

RECORD ATTENDEE TESTIMONIALS

SPEAKER TIP #39:

Make the time to record brief video testimonials from "raving fans" in your audiences. Following your speeches, there will typically be people in the audience who your message resonates with deeply enough that they become instant "raving fans". Leverage the impact you made through your speech by having these individuals to record a 1-2 minute testimonial video right onsite. Focus the testimony on their takeaways from your speech, the impact, and the action they plan to take afterwards. Then, upload the testimonials onto your website and in your digital speaker marketing materials as a form of added credibility.

NOTE: Whenever possible, request a video testimonial while onsite from the planner/organizer who hired you and other senior level personnel who experienced your presentation.

SPEAKER TIP #40:

CUSTOMIZE AND PERSONALIZE IT

SPEAKER TIP #40:

Organizations, associations, and groups who hire you to speak do not want a cookie-cutter presentation. They want you to customize your message and personalize the experience for their group – engage their audience, speak their language, know their pain points, and stress the right message with appropriate stories. Although speaking to small or large groups, it is always your job to customize your content and present it in a personalized way that makes each participant feel like you are talking to them individually. You will know you have hit the mark when your audience wants the outcome you have presented because they will see themselves in you and want the same outcome you have achieved.

NOTE: The best compliment a speaker can receive from an attendee is: "I felt like you were talking directly to me."

SPEAKER TIP #41:

CREATE PRODUCTS

SPEAKER TIP #41:

Create ways for people who experience you from the stage to also "take a piece of you home" by developing products and services they can purchase after your speech. This will extend and expand their learning. There are five major avenues of learning – (i) reading, (ii) hearing, (iii) seeing, (iv) experiencing and (v) mastering – that you can leverage for your audiences to learn from you. Your products and services can include books, cds, dvds, workbooks, video series, digital training, masterminds, coaching, and live events.

Create A Plan Of Action:
- What product(s) do I have to offer attendees to purchase after they hear me speak?
- What service(s)/program(s) do I have to offer attendees to purchase after they hear me speak?
- Do I have a live or virtual event that I can promote after I speak?

SPEAKER TIP #42:

BE RELATABLE

SPEAKER TIP #42:

One of the best ways to deepen your connection as a speaker is to allow the audience to "see themselves in you." That requires a level of vulnerability on your part to share some of the challenges, setbacks, obstacles, and roadblocks you have personally experienced in your own journey as it relates to the topic you are presenting. Always remember that your story (your unique experiences) becomes your instant *connector* with the audience. Then, your success becomes your *credibility* with the audience.

Reflect on these questions:
- What have I struggled through in the past, and overcome, that my audience is currently struggling with?
- What lessons did I learn through my process that I can share with my audience to benefit them?
- What successes can I share with the audience to show them that overcoming this struggle is possible?
- What solutions can I offer the audience that will help them to take steps to move forward now?

SPEAKER TIP #43:

GROW YOUR VISIBILITY

SPEAKER TIP #43:

"Visibility will get your foot in the door, Credibility will keep it there." (Cheryl Wood)

Visibility and Credibility are equally important in your speaking business. You must be **viewed** as an expert in order to get **booked and paid** as an expert. To increase your visibility, take advantage of every opportunity to educate and inform your target audience from an "expert" perspective – social media posts, newsletters, expert articles, podcasts, webinars, radio/television interviews. Develop a level of consistency that keeps you visible, then OVERDELIVER on every platform – live or digital – to solidify your credibility!

SPEAKER TIP #44:

DIVERSIFY YOUR REVENUE

SPEAKER TIP #44:

Do not put all of your eggs in one basket as a professional speaker. It is critical that you DIVERSIFY and incorporate multiple streams of revenue into your speaking business. Some speakers make the mistake of assuming that the bulk of their revenue will be generated from PAID speaking engagements, however, the biggest secret in the speaker industry is that many successful speakers (6-figure and 7-figure speakers) generate more revenue from "Back of the room" sales than from paid speaking. "Back of the room sales" refers to a sales offer you make to attendees from the stage and they meet you in the back of the room to say "yes" to investing in your offer. When packaged and positioned strategically, you have the potential to earn your full speakers fee (and much more) from "Back of the room" sales.

SPEAKER TIP #45:

BE PASSIONATE

SPEAKER TIP #45:

Be passionate about your topic(s) and show that passion! As a professional speaker, you should have a strong stance on whatever topic(s) you choose to speak about. Allow the audience to see how much you care about your topic. When you genuinely care about your topic, the enthusiasm and passion with which you deliver your message will shine through. It will ignite the interest of the audience and that enthusiasm and passion will become contagious for everyone who experiences it, moving them to want to take action.

Ask Yourself:
- What topic(s) am I most passionate about?
- How do I demonstrate my passion for this topic(s) when I am speaking on stage?
- Do I share personal stories that demonstrate my connection to the topic(s)?

SPEAKER TIP #46:

KEEP LEARNING

SPEAKER TIP #46:

Continue being a student of your craft as a speaker. Don't ever presume that you have "arrived" and no longer need to learn and grow. The reality is: the more you learn and grow, the more valuable you become to organizations that want to book and pay you for your expertise as well as to clients who want to hire you to learn what you know. Keep investing in yourself through coaching programs, mentorship programs, masterminds, conferences, books, and other learning products that help you to continue sharpening your craft.

Ask Yourself:

- What was the last investment I made in myself as an emerging speaker?
- Have my investments in myself been equivalent to the level of investments I offer to my clients?
- What are the last 4 books I have read to sharpen my craft as a speaker?

SPEAKER TIP #47:

CREATE RELEVANT TITLES

SPEAKER TIP #47:

Give deep thought to your speech titles. Brainstorm on relevant and compelling titles that will grab your audience's attention. Remember that your speech titles will be used when you are introduced to the stage, will appear in the event program or agenda, and will be used to attract a larger audience to your speech. Your titles require the same creative effort as every other part of your preparation as a speaker. Your title can be a teaser to your content or the structure of your speech, can focus on a problem or a solution, or can plant an assumption to add emphasis to your message.

Make sure your titles are clear, relevant, and intriguing!

SPEAKER TIP #48:

BELIEVE IN YOUR VALUE

SPEAKER TIP #48:

In order to articulate the value you deliver as a professional speaker, you must BELIEVE in the value you deliver. You must acknowledge the overwhelming impact and transformation that your message creates in the world and develop a crazy-glue commitment to sharing it. Continue increasing your belief as a speaker by upgrading your daily internal dialogue. Only speak positive words that lead to positive thoughts and actions.

Your subconscious mind will only believe what you repeatedly tell yourself, so remind yourself daily that:

"MY VOICE AS A SPEAKER MATTERS!"

SPEAKER TIP #49:

FOLLOW THE FORMULA

SPEAKER TIP #49:

To become an impactful speaker who is repeatedly booked and paid to speak, your speeches must always follow the "**Speech Success Formula**" below:

- Contain quality content
- Be timely, relevant, and relatable
- Be interactive and engaging
- Have practical, easy-to-implement strategies
- Promote positive change to improve people's lives
- Contain compelling stories
- Include versatile learning styles
- Have identifiable and measurable takeaways
- Include a clear Call-To-Action

SPEAKER TIP #50:

THINK ABUNDANTLY

SPEAKER TIP #50:

There are over 7.6 Billion people in the world which means **THERE IS ENOUGH FOR YOU!** Do not throw away valuable time diminishing the expertise you bring to the speaking industry, questioning whether or not there are already too many people speaking about the same topic you want to speak about, or comparing yourself to anyone else in the industry. You have a UNIQUE PERSPECTIVE, that cannot be duplicated, on the topic(s) of your choice. Take full ownership of your perspective based on your knowledge and unique experiences and boldly share that perspective without letup!

Somebody is waiting for your message!!

CONGRATULATIONS!

Congratulations on purchasing this valuable speaker resource! You have made the conclusive decision to be intentional about improving your speaking skills and mastering the art of making an unforgettable impact on the world with your unique message.

Just like you, I acknowledge that, in order to grow, we must become life-long learners and take consistent action to gain mastery over the skill sets we want to share with the world.

My mission with the circulation of this book is to empower and equip individuals globally who have a desire to make a positive impact on the world through the power of their voice, perspective, message, and story with core . Now is your time to go out into the world and SPEAK!

NEVER FORGET:

"Get out into the world and powerfully share your voice because somebody needs what you know RIGHT NOW!" (Cheryl Wood)

NEXT STEPS. . .

Are you an organizer or planner trusted with the responsibility of finding talented, engaging speakers for your company's events?

Are you are a new, aspiring, or emerging speaker seeking speaker development training? Ready to unveil your unique story, develop your signature speech, and get booked and paid to speak?

For more information about Booking Cheryl to speak or Hiring Cheryl for speaker training:

CALL:
301-395-7589

EMAIL:
Assistant@cherylwoodempowers.com